P9-AGI-875

THE HARD ESSENTIAL LANDSCAPE

WITHDRAWN
UTSA LIBRARIES

University of Central Florida

Contemporary Poetry Series

Other works in the series:

Malcolm Glass, *Bone Love*
Susan Hartman, *Dumb Show*
David Posner, *The Sandpipers*
Edmund Skellings, *Heart Attacks*
Edmund Skellings, *Face Value*

THE HARD ESSENTIAL LANDSCAPE

POEMS

by

Van K. Brock

A University of Central Florida Book

UNIVERSITY PRESSES OF FLORIDA
FAMU/FAU/FIU/FSU/UCF/UF/UNF/USF/UWF
Orlando

Copyright © 1965, 1966, 1967, 1968, 1970, 1971, 1972, 1973, 1974, 1975, 1976, 1977, 1978, 1979 by Van K. Brock

All rights reserved

Printed in Florida

University Presses of Florida, the agency of the State of Florida's university system for the publication of scholarly and creative works, operates under policies adopted by the Board of Regents. Its offices are located at 15 Northwest 15th Street, Gainesville, Florida 32603.

Library of Congress Cataloging in Publication Data

Brock, Van K.
   The hard essential landscape.

   (University of Central Florida contemporary poetry series) (A University of Central Florida book)
   I. Title. II. Series: Contemporary poetry series (Orlando, Fla.)
PS3552.R614H3   811´.5´4   79-21071
ISBN 0-8130-0659-7

LIBRARY
**The University of Texas
At San Antonio**

Printed by Storter Printing Company
Gainesville, Florida

Cover drawing by William C. Henderson (Galerie Internationale
1095 Madison Avenue, New York NY 10028)

Acknowledgments

The author thanks the original publishers for permission to reprint the poems in this collection:

"Apalachee" and "Remembering Dresden" first appeared in a special issue of *New Collage*; copyright 1978 by New Collage. "Driving at Dawn" and "Cows Walking in a Pasture" are reprinted by permission of *Your Grace*. "The Horses" originally appeared in the Kansas City *Star* as winner of the H. Jay Sharp Award in the College Division of the Heart of America Contests, 1964; reprinted by permission of the Kansas City *Star-Times*. "The Moth" and "The Sea Birds" were both first published in *The New Yorker*. "For the Injured Squirrel Found on Centerville Road," "Bellair," and "Lake Country White" appeared originally in *Poets in the South*; "The Mockingbird," "The Aucilla," "The Key," and "The Tree" in *Gryphon*; "The Absurd Snowman" in *The Back Door*; "Sassafras," "Childhood," and "The Land of Old Fields" in *Florida Review*.

"The View from My Hammock," was first printed by Iris Press of Binghamton, N.Y. (May 1979). "Landscapes for Voyagers" was first published by *The Yale Review*.

"The Posthumous Son: The Deathbirth" and "King" are reprinted by permission of *Southern Poetry Review*; the former first appeared as "The Deathbirth" in a special anthology issue, *Southern Poetry: The Seventies*.

"France, October, 1918" first appeared in *Shenandoah*. "The Lookout" and "Ostraka" were first published by Burnt Hickory Press in *Weighing the Penalties*, by Van K. Brock.

"The Ceremonies" was first published in *Sewanee Review* 82 (Summer 1974). Copyright 1974 by the University of the South. Reprinted by permission of the editor.

"Spelunking" was originally published by Louisiana State University Press in *Southern Writing in the Sixties*, edited by John Corrington and Miller Williams.

"Dead Man Creek," "The Fans," and "Littoral" were originally published in *North American Review*. "Rites: Nightfishing," "The Book of the Dead," "The Ivory-Billed Woodpecker," and "In the Manner of V. B." first appeared in *Southern Review*.

"The Dreamers" was first published by Abbey Press in *I love you all day, it is that simple*, edited by Philip Dacey and Gerald Knoll.

"In the Zebra" is reprinted by permission of *Prairie Schooner*, copyright 1972 by the University of Nebraska Press. "The Lives and Wars of Bunzo Minagawa" first appeared in *Quarterly Review of Literature*.

"Sightings: Ivory-Billed Woodpecker" and "The Dead Baby" first appeared in *Apalachee Quarterly*. "The Tunnel" first appeared in the Atlanta *Gazette*. "Christ in the Sun," "The Turtle's Voice," and "To a Friend" first appeared in *Skullpolish*. "The Evidence" and "Federal Pen" first appeared in *Georgia Review*.

*For my grandmother and my mother
and for my wife and our children*

Contents

1

Apalachee

Sea licked, lapped it, then fell back,
leaving Apalachee dry tide land.

South:

> a sandy plain of palmetto
> cabbage palm and scrub oak
> scattered in pinewoods.
> (Along rivers and in swamps
> of map turtle and cottonmouth
> sheltered by yaupon and bay,
> the snakebird perches,
> drying spread wings,
> and ponders the sunken sky.)

North:

> green-brushed gray hills
> hiding red clay
> that lids limestone skeletons
> of a petrified desert, older
> than vegetation.
> (Water
> has riddled it with caves.
> It swallows rivers
> and spews them out.)

East:

> Wacissa, Aucilla, Suwannee—
> rivers moving in and out
> of the earth in their seams.

Midmost:

> Wakulla,
> rising from deep water tables
> holding in museum rooms
> the pottery, carvings and tools
> of men whose bones are guarded
> by bones of beasts older than man:
> only the transparency rising
> into the river,
> Wakulla,
> crossed by a chain-link fence.

West:

> Apalachicola, the unitary tongue
> of four rivers stammering toward
> one mouth as the landscape
> slopes toward blue gulf

While Chipola echoes in its caves a Mass
for bats, crayfish and blind, pink salamanders.

Driving at Dawn

A dead rabbit by the roadside,
Sunlight turning his ears to rose petals.

A new electric fence,
Its five barbed wires tight
As a steel-stringed banjo.

The feet of a fat dove
On a high black line
Throbbing to the hum
Of a thousand waterfalls.

A flock of egrets in a field of cows.

Three Great Blue Herons like hunchbacked
    pelicans in a watering pond.

The red leaves of a bush
Burning inside me.

A swamp holding its breath.

Sightings: Ivory-Billed Woodpecker

Too quick in the new light,
A large bird flashed above the car
As I drove southeast at six a.m.
Through woods on a narrow road.

Before he vanished, the fleshy
Ivory-bill was a delicacy rare as our
Great rattlesnakes or freshwater cats.
He circles above us.

Later that day, miles to the north
I spotted his pileated cousin
On a tree not fifty feet off
The highway south of Quitman, Ga.

o, dumb brilliance, you who lay your egg
or two only in the deepest forest, who
tend your young too long, and who
when the drums beat faster can not
change your diet, will not,
can not, when the forest is pillaged
of your deadwood worm-farms and roosts,
adapt to a new niche, o dumb brilliance

In 1951 two birds, perhaps not mates,
Were reported in northern Florida.
Believers still search for survivors
Amid rumors of verified sightings
Naturalists will not announce,
Their feathers and beaks prized
By the Indians and collectors.

Head-on, my grill has eaten
Swallows, bluejays, owls,
And a million love-bugs locked
In death-grip copulations.

Circling, circling.

Cows Waking in a Pasture

Black and white splotches
on a ground of dull green
space themselves
with the precise irregularity
of their own patterns.
They have carefully varied
their postures and positions
to their own needs.

One is raising her head
and opening her eyes.
One is stretched out
on her side, still asleep.
Another has been lying
on a hummock all night
and is trying, awkwardly,
to raise herself,
hooves in the air.
One by one they will
mock her motions.

The Horses

Overtaking a
Double horsetrailer,
I can see only
The ears and rears of
The two horses. One
Has his tail tucked in
The tailgate; one tail
Hangs out. The beige tails
Contrast with chestnut
Flanks. Because they are
Alike, the contrast
Makes them both appear
Misshapen. Somewhere
Between, their one form
Blurs and won't focus;
For slight differences
Become the movements
Of horses running
Diagonally
Opposite ways in
Airy arenas
Containing only
Horse torn by horses.

And now though I can't
Put a rein on God,
I feel him tearing
Between the horses
And myself, for we
Are in separate
Vehicles, each one
Moving fast. I pass,
Hills and curves moving.

The Moth

He spins himself into a dark inscape.
Poor worm, still turning in that shroud, he fights
The dissolution of form and keeps outrageous
Traces of battering color, warmth, and light.

Turning, he fuses the threads into tough membranes;
His pushing toward the light scars them with paints.
And through his turning—craftsman, craft, and lathe—
The caterpillar frees the inner moth.

The crumpled wings unfold and season; the moth
Beats light into color, flight into form
(Himself the flame, smokeless and unconsumed).
Concrete, abstract, he moves at once in both.

For the Injured Squirrel Found on Centerville Road

I thought you were a dead rat (you looked so small)
And turned around and went back
For the sake of the healed gray rat snake
I had rescued (jaw dislocated)
A month before from the same racetrack.
You grew, reproaching me with your life
(Hyperventilating, nose to asphalt, eyes black beads).

Drivers went warily around me.

I put you on the back floorboard,
Hoping to arrive home with a small warm corpse.
Now my sons have betrayed their snake
With the same fervor that held on to his rights
(They will let nothing go since the blue jay died).
Even in their dreams they try to enter
Your dreams and hold on to your breath.

You do not understand the rules
Of "protective custody." With water and grain
And a nest of cotton balls in an old styrofoam
Picnic cooler covered with hardware-cloth screen,
You have everything going for you.
But as soon as the room is empty of sound
You begin to scratch away at your walls.
(I did not want you to be my captive
Any more than you wanted to be.)

I tell Geoff and Brant that there is little to do
For one with a broken leg
Who would rather be dead than a prisoner
Of our patronage. Perhaps I should have
Given you a chance with the cats outside
Who perpetually leave food in their bowls
Rather than relinquish entirely the edge of hunger.

After you died we let the rat snake go.

The Mockingbird

Enraged by a red crest,
A cardinal, his own rival,
Battered our sliding doors
Until he broke himself
Of illusion, striving.

The yellow-throated warbler
Also shattered his glass eye.

But the mockingbird who lately
Mated and nested in our sylvestrus
Now in the first chill of autumn
Woos with daily diligence
The unlikely bird
Locked in our bedroom window.

I draw and undraw the drape.
Turn the light on and off.
Still he sees his gray
Recessive self.
Chak Chak Chak
Again he flies to the glass
And beats his wings against it.

Only my approach from within
Sends him to a near branch
Where he perches and offers
His cubist musical crest
To the form that for
A moment dissolved in me.

The Lookout

Drowned in bug spray
And shrouded in sleeping bags,
We lie in our high fort
Like dead Plains Indians on a burial platform,
Tall posts lifting slat walls into air,
My sleeping sons stolen by dreams.

While twenty houses blink,
Fireflies and frogcalls
Pulse in the night.
Far-off housewives glide
Past veiled glassdoors.

We sway on calloused trees.
Each of us sheds his skin
To enter a damp hole in dark grass and wait
(Eyes close to the ground)
For mouse, rabbit, toad
To come into the quick
Mouths of nothing, caves of nothing.

My sons change forms through the night,
Move through interstices of grass,
Becoming their pets—snapper, lizard, frog;
They enter grub and caterpillar
And mount above the bug spray
As nocturnal butterfly and locust.
They devour what they are,
Nothing, visible or invisible, too small to be prey.
They have tackled the small kingdoms.

* * *

The rain begins gently on tattered banana leaves.
The plants drink with their pores.
All appetite, they fold their sex in their blooms,
Half of them grown from cuttings from roots or stems.
Bamboo, elephant ears, azaleas, Joseph's coat—
Their names rise like song from the ground
My wife has stirred
For jasmine, pyrocantha, catalpa, althea, wisteria—

The names of goddesses, daughters of earth.
If I did not cut them back they would swallow
This house in a mere summer and bury it in vines
With leaves as large as fans to ventilate the moist beds.

I cry this house hugging its plot
Half-set into the hillside that rises from my left
And slopes away from my right;
I cry the cycles of day and night that hold it,
The season of rain and sun, of growing and dying,
And every plot a little wilderness
We work, with ignorance or knowing.
                    I stay in my yard
                          and penetrate this night,
My wife in bed alone.

The Aucilla

East of Tallahassee
Dick Ohmes dives into the Aucilla
a mile below where it spouts
out of wet dirt walls,
the whole weight of air riding it
upward. He has crawled for miles
over that river-bottom
and into its unlit caves
in his wet-suit and mask.

From the map of the riverbed in his head,
he draws the bottom with a corrugated
line, intermittent ridges,
low underwater dams
defining small shallow basins.
In one of these he has found
two mammoth skeletons,
a saber-tooth skull,
the tibia of a giant sloth,
arrowheads and bone tools.

"The tiger skull you saw in my
studio was a cast of the giant
jaguar, *felix atrox,* found in
the Ichetucknee River by
the son of Ross Allen, the
herpetologist. *Felix atrox* was
half again larger than a modern
lion. No saber-tooth skull,
only fragments." (Ohmes)

Tannic acid from cypress roots steeps
the water the color of weak tea.
Gnarled wood, long sunken and preserved
in airless silts, turns black as teak
and never rots. For Ohmes, an intact
archaeological core from this riverbottom
would be a lighted window
in walls older than Crete.

Even in droughts there remains
some cool dark veil of water. Once
the sea came to the edge of this basin.
"Greece and Rome," he begins,
wearily, on archaeologists;
"Still others around," he says quietly,
"think only of brass buttons,
minnie balls, federal coins.
Froth on the wave."

He descends again into the cold current.
Dick Ohmes is the mind of that river;
it runs through Dick Ohmes' mind; in it
he has survived a Ph.D. in psychology
from Vienna, research on physics
and days farming near Chaires.
In it he hears the hum of high pines
and cypresses, the quiet of primeval
forests where the giant sloth towered.

He raises his hand in an arc
taller than his barn, showing me
the great sloth, his footfall shaking
the ground, and beyond, reduced by this,
a mammoth shrinks behind an oak
whose branches, heavy with hanging moss,
drag the ground as if remembering
a saber-tooth under a thicket
snarling like a challenged god.

The vegetation meets dim shadows;
continents drifting apart, through slow eons,
create seas with distance—and this side
of the giant animals, the shadow of man,
spreading. The man haunts him most.
He tries to get inside him. He has learned
to make his clovis points, tools and pots,
played with his skull, tried to see

from those sockets, built up a replica
with clay, earth color, painted him
walking through virginal swamplands,
a youth, 5′ 10″ weighing 160 lbs., moving
so quietly only Ohmes can follow his faint
footprints through needling thickets of holly,
cabbage palm, pine, woven with blackberry
and bamboo vines.

Ohmes, rising from the deep cold water
to rub himself to warmth again, from a distance
looks like his paleoman, reborn over and over
from the buried river.

The Absurd Snowman

". . . Time is where he is. . . ."

"The snowman, what can it be?
Mockery of death
or mockery of life?"
Edwin S. Godsey (1930-1967)

Who drowned trying to save his son
who had fallen through the ice.

Where snowmen tame wild country
there is a river, deep
in the laughter of children
where you have swum
far from the hole in the ice
and beyond all possibles
to show the singing rainbow trout
     to your son.

We see how, fused by impulse,
we might have entered that zero
for strangers; in howling wind,
we cavil at feet kicking
numbly against indulgent water
till the head cracks
on a frozen sky. Striate
     with doubt,

We defer to one who defines us
in doing what no father could not,
facing such cold. For since,
beyond all doubt, it was yourself
you sought, as saints their souls,
or a quail-cock flying between
hawk and chick, your definition holds
    an old rhythm,

Showing us something of ourselves
hoarded for dread necessities from
daily affairs. You have escaped
from the currents of the one-eyed lake
through the eye of untraced veins,
an absurd snowman, bearing your son
in your arms, our sons to us, our selves
    to our sons.

The Sea Birds

No light except the stars, but from the cliff
I saw in motion, out on the rolling waves,
The white sea birds that swim beyond the surf.

Their movements made a pattern on the mauve,
Contorted stretch of cold, corrosive water,
Where even the images of stars dissolve.

When I had thought the birds were fixed in order,
I saw the swimming rim of their starlit ring
Minutely swerve and spiral toward the center!

The birds that had been swimming in between
Were shuttled outward on a wheel of light,
Reflecting, like the sea, the star's design.

I paused, and looked, and saw a star burn out
And sink back into space as through a fissure.
It was an ancient word without a thought.

Perhaps birds move in pattern for the measure
It imposes on the ruptured waves at night;
Perhaps they spiral purely for their pleasure.

While I was trying to untie this knot,
A motion in the motion of the weather
Turned, and the birds turned too and tore the net

I knitted for them (a star had torn another
I had knitted for stars). I saw them climb the gale
That drove small arrows in through every feather—

One by one they spread their flapping sails.
I think the stars are moving in a school
With restless birds above a freezing pool,
And no one shall put salt on their bright tails.

Sassafras

Its leaves have fingers.
Together they are a thousand green veils
whispering around the face of nothing.
In a strong wind, it sings.
Creek made tea
from its roots.
I chew it, slightly sweet
mixed with musk.
Its fragrance opens doors
into other dimensions,
the tap of root beer
waiting cold in earth.
A black man said, "If ya
cut down a sassafras some one'll die."
I found the limb of a tree,
one shoot right angle to the main,
chewed as I whittled,
had five visions,
made a cane with a bent
handle.

The View from My Hammock

The pines look smooth and straight
From a distance, but when I lie
In my hammock stretched between two
Pines, I look up at configurations
Where lightning hit the one at my
Feet and cry out, "God! God!"

Resin has healed it against rot
And insects. Limbs are broken
Where I pulled off strangling
Kudzu. Dead vines hang higher up.
There are no limbs on one side.
The tree at its back blocked light.

Its bark tells it is cracked by
Its own growth. Its bare side is
The back of a man sealed in wood.
Arms reach out. The tree groans.
I try to imagine it stuttering
A flawed rune in its wooden tongue.

The tree at my head is almost as
Tortured. Birds scallop the breeze
Into quilts of air that will never be
Seen. They have resurgence in their
Veins. I close my eyes, sway the thin
Net of nylon tight with my weight.

The trees feel the weight and hold
Me between them. Idiot saints
Miming to God. A bird lights. I know
Him by his tail feathers as the one
The cat almost got. And the tip
Of his beak has been blunted.

Landscapes for Voyagers

Sailing to north without a word for winter,
We docked our hollow ships and moved inland,
In search of new worlds, toward this temperate region
Where foliage hid the land as in the tropics.

Though the summer was as hot as any other,
Whatever autumn asked for with its color
Was answered only by the animals,
Who understood the language of the weather.

Winter is the hard, essential landscape.
Cold, reassuring our sick, we move toward seas,
Not knowing whether there is any ship that goes
Where we desire, ready to challenge all captains.

2

The Posthumous Son:
The Deathbirth

In the hot night, I hear him
Cry through the thrush. The thread
Of his life muscles through me.
The light of his body's sweat
Walks ahead in the dark,
While his rising fever stretches
Then slowly contracts my head.

When I first passed from him
Into his other body
I was the warmth of winter
And still half-boy, half-girl,
Floated in the milklight
Half-world, curling
Myself in his fever.
                                    There,
His mother's death at six,
Midwife of his mind's birth,
Still throbbed his infant thoughts.
My mother's memories swirl dreams
With dried records and crumbling
Letters.
                  The dust settles.
Father and son of these confusions,
Older than you were,
I know you
As you never knew yourself.

France, October, 1918

Illuminated at night
By the bleeding lights of mortar
And sometimes at day
By the green-yellow gas,
You are running: I see you weaving,
Your white hubcap-helmet
With a red cross on each side
Bouncing as you dance beneath flares,
Nothing between you and death
But a field of chance and discipline.
You are running on a swiss-cheese moon.
Then you are coming toward me,
Crawling on your belly like a snake
With a wounded man on your back,
While I cheer you on—half hoping
To see your features at last.
But the lights exploding above you
Behind your head
Leave your face in that dark
That lies between us
Full of trenches and barbed wire.
When you have crawled so near
I think you have crawled
From the earth, from the grave,
For a glimpse of the son
You never saw, I almost whisper—
Something—"Father?"—"Arthur?"—
A flare falls between us
Washing that field with light
To reveal you like an insect,

Gas mask on your face,
Glass eyes shooting light
As you sink in the stinking trench,
And it breaks on me
That the wounded man on your back
Swallowed with you in the trench,
Is me, and that whoever he was
Or might have been is dead,
And you lie in the tent, with fever,
Though the war is over.

Ostraka

My father left me a dark sea chest
(Stencilled with his name and serial number)
Containing an empty grenade; a length of bamboo
From Cuba, four inches thick with one end hollow;
A tin mess-kit with canteen; and odds-
And-ends.
        I played with them; they were more real
Than the picture on the mantle, everything in shades
Of brown, the background darker than the uniform,
And features firm despite their dark modelling.

He built the house and barn and, near the woods,
Dug the graves of his stillborn son and daughter,
And when my brother lived, my father laughed
Thoughout the indebted land. Then, mother pregnant,
He died.
        The doctor, who had prescribed hot pads,
Said he was full of pus. My mother, in lasting
Shock, wondered afterwards if they left him
Open. The doctor agreed to take the truck
In payment for the operation—and my birth.

My brother and I played on the pebbled graves.

I remember the new room Grandfather built on
The unpainted house, the unfaded yellow pine
Against the gray. In the dirt yard,
Scratched clean by the gallberry brooms, I ranged
Between the smokehouse, woodpile and toolshed,
The fields and the woods. At night, on the backporch,
I listened to the dogs barking at the owls.

It was there that my brother's cat I tortured
With love went wild and never came back nearer
Than the hedge and that but once, there that plodding
Chance, with hooves like saucers, stepped on my
Pink pig.
            Then came my uncles, huge with youth,
Who, walking with guns and dogs into nightwoods
Promising an owl, woke me from my broken
Watch to boast of the screechless softness on
The kitchen floor.

                        When Grandfather died, propped up
In the front room, with the whole family there
To watch, his eyes fell closed and his toothless mouth
Fell open. My cousins and I shrilled in the yard.

They called us in to make us cry, as though
This were the ceremony. But, my eyes full
Of sand, I watched them putting pennies on his
And, with my cousins, went back to our play.

The Ceremonies

It was our best festival.
Always in high summer,
On Grandpa's birthday, together,
Aunts, uncles, and cousins
Loaded car trunks and trucks
With tools, lunch, ice tea,
And drove to the cemetery
To clean around the graves.
And hearing again who this
Or that one was, we tried
To draw from old folks' minds
A girl our age, who played
With our own mothers, and dead
Brothers and sisters who looked
Like our own baby pictures.

Though cousins married outside,
Our square lot's low curb barred
Some ten acres of dead.
We children strayed toward graves
Of children or revisited
Old dirt mounds without stones,
New graves with wilted flowers,
And always ended at the oldest
Whose concrete top, caved
In, had once arched, but now
Some worn-out dates, a dash,
Broken on the name.

We thought he was our lost
Grandfather, the cavity almost
Hidden by a red cedar
Whose brown needles covered
The bones as the tree and the man
Mixed in one grave with
Rain, this continent and
What we wanted him to be—
Red skin, leathered, wiser,
Not to live or rise
Again but always to be there,
The Indian on the nickel
In our pockets, the one we matched with
And had not yet spent, the father
We dispossessed in the common
Grave of repressed dreams.

Death's dull uniform
Dwarfed obelisks crusted
With marble birds faceless
Angels shepherds woolly
Lambs blur like dulled
Poppies in a distant field
We hurried past, returning
To the motions of living parents—
Her there, kneeling beside
His grave cupping a mound
Of dirt around the flowering
Vine winding the cross stone.
She would raise one knee to rise,

Stop to weed around
The edges, rise, then stoop
To pull a handful of sage
From the hedge. I wondered
If she thought that through
His slab the bonedust knew,
And if he still decayed.

Only the sun's rays
Credible, we cleaned the curb
And fence, raked, cropped,
Found a turtle egg the ground
Exposed, gray leather time
Capsule we put on the cool
Meeting house pulpit and forced
In a house without locks
Where no one lived and only
The illicit made love,
Then held a somber service
For the fetus of one turtle.
This cradle was his tomb
And though he was not old
He is shrivelled. Brother,
This was our brother; Sister,
Your child. We all hummed
A hymn in the hot afternoon
As we laid it in the sunless ground,
In the turtle's heart, and mine,
Where at times he still turns
Grandpa's beaked but blank face
Toward being, then turns it away.

Spelunking

I killed the useless light,
  And, fingers like snakes,
Crawled in hilly darkness.
   Earth's dark touched inside
Defied proportion. Shelves
   Dissolved. Stoning depths,
I splashed hidden rivers—
   Knowing of no hell,
That all circles nightmare,
   That panic crumbles
Earth. My leather whispers,
   Carousing like bats,
Echoed their own beings.
   Rules say sit and wait,
But this crazy cave kept
   Combing the cool earth.

In light's forgotten roots
  A headless hill bled
With a blue silver blaze,
   And by its streams where
Orchards sprang from hidden
   Fruits, animals grazed.
While Father searched earth, his
   Sun burning on his
Brow, there at last the sun
   And moon together
Shoaled my still-born sister,
   With a slight friend (struck
In youth by lightning) who

Played with my dogs, names
Forgotten, including
        The six-week puppy
My brother killed in wrath.
        We were all strangers,
Our lives over our heads.

Though the sounds of bats grew
        Slowly to cries and
I decided they were
        Not my own lost sounds,
I did not answer the
        Rescue crew at first.
My name in a stranger's
        Mouth was wrong, my voice
Echo to them whose hands
        Were colder than life;
And flesh in their lanterns,
        Even mine, was not
A known color. The roots
        Began to dissolve
In slow shock waves of day,
        And I felt myself
Swimming against the light
        Toward people who cheered
When I emerged, although
        They did not know what
I had found in earth; I
        Was a stranger. They
        Looked for themselves or
Something they had buried.

Dead Man Creek

The water was usually clean
where the river backed upstream
to receive Dead Man Creek,
but we swam out and dived
from anchored inner tubes
for tires, luggage and books.
Skins sealed with semen
floated. Gar, cottonmouth
and gators were sighted. Once
we netted a bloated human
fetus our fingers dissolved
at touch. But I still have
Williams' "The Wanderer," a water-
warped *Aeneid,* and one
work in the original Greek.

We hung a tire from a limb
over the cove, dried
the books in a driftboard
treehouse, and swung above
the water. We fished with hooks
and nets (gloved hands for cats),
then afterward washed in the stream
beneath the waterfall
and ate our kill and catch,
telling dirty jokes,
talking of cock like virgins.

By a sinking sun we dredged
enormities from each other
with stories: I remember the panthers
crouching in dark shadows
(half-cat, half-human; no way
to tell the real), swaying
with limbs and sounding like beautiful
women distressed. Waiting.
Wanting to bring you to them.
We believed it all. Each
heard the sound in himself.
So real was Albert's scream
that a startled mockingbird picked up
the cry from the telling to make
a song of our terror, repeating
it purely, repeatedly. Those nights
we headed home, sure
that we would not get there,
weighing the penalties.

Rites: Nightfishing

When, with flashlights,
We waded in the night swamp,
The boys and their fathers,
Both with rifles,
And I with my striking iron,
I came on a sheepshead, asleep.
His wide black and white stripes
(That would have hidden him
In sunlight among the shadows
Of limbs) gave him to me.
He lay there in his dream
Of the solid dark
While I raised my arm
And swift as a shock
Fused his dream with steel,
Making him part of mine.
He was day and night. We ate him.

Childhood

In the late midsummer we made
A biplane from a railroad tie
Fuselage and two 2 x 12 wings
To fight red-eyed Dog Days
Bearing down like Zeroes. As we
Added elevator and rudder, I began
To believe my cousin and I could
Climb over his house, old garage,
And even the town and county
Straddling that solid beam. I
Had never made such flights and
Was too old; but for a moment
I made that nailed wood fly.

There in front of the garage
Where we worked as the hurt pup
Bit each nail, the sore by its
Ear breathed. And when we looked
Closely, in it, dispersed, swam
Alive on his life, in his, his
Death—maggots! Error past repair.
Horror, duty, regret, remorse—
Name it. Vets were far from us.
Folks said, "poor-thing-must-be-
Killed." With no gun, unable to
Bring ourselves to smash his head,
We dug a hole and covered him up,
                    instead.

The Fans

In summer, the sound of the large window
Fans that circulate the heat
Vibrates our bodies and we unwind.

The whirring propeller that stirs the air
Around one calms the currents inside.
I almost sleep in my hard chair,

As though beneath the huge black blades
That swung above my head as a child,
Circling a pipe from the ceiling until

I feel a draft from where there is
No skylight; and I look up as though
In the shops of childhood's small town

And see a long fluorescent tube
As bright as the street where horses were hitched
To wagons beside old cars in shades.

A fly walks up the naked light
As a dust cloud comes from the end of town.
The barber, the druggist—through the back door.

That one-street movie set becomes
Africa, Asia, and Arabia while
The French and English in khaki shorts

Are ordering cokes, as the black fans
Turn slowly overhead, dissolving
Them and the day and the whole summer.

I sit here hypnotized, my head
Spinning in the shrivelling heat, my will,
Suspended, struggling to stay awake.

I hold to the present, although I hear
The blacksmith of the thirties pounding
An anvil, disturbing the fading curtain

With a rhythm that neither begins nor ceases.
In his open shed, I see him standing
By an open forge, where the huddled summers

Generate all the world's factories,
Hung with the huge fans, those rimless
Wheels that turn around themselves.

They draw a current of distilled matter
From the veins of pure fire,
Waiting to be replaced by the smooth

Almost silent hum of the air
Conditioners and finally a cool silence—
With the engine in the basement or the back yard.

Remembering Dresden (2/13—15/1945)

(The British had learned a technique
for placing bombs to create firestorms.
The Russians were approaching Dresden.)

Dresdener:

British reconnaissance planes
Dropped flares called "Christmas trees"
To mark the target.

At ten o'clock the first bombers
Dropped explosive bombs.
People evacuated the downtown.

Our street was filled.
At two, the firebombs caught them
Sleeping, some in tents, in the open.

St. Valentine's day and the next,
American bombers pounded the ruins.

Blackened bodies shrunken to babies
Lay at the doors of churches and cellars
Or at curbs had clawed with fingernails
For shelter in the hollows of gutters.

The Frauenkirche, the Semper Galerie,
The Zwinger Museum—gutted.
A hundred major monuments smoldering.

The structure of time torn.

Forty hospitals in the eye of the firestorm.

Eight nights.
Glowing columns of smoke three miles high.
A valentine for Stalin.

Dutch Prisoner:

A nerve center for the Reich,
Its industry made complex systems,
Its intelligence served insanity.

We went through the Florence-on-the-Elbe,
Five months before the bombing,
Past their last great

Railway-engine repair works
Working furiously. To us,
It was already the trainworks of hell.

They said we were going a bit north,
To Riesa's steelworks as slave laborers.
We were in three trains,

Sixty to a boxcar,
Fifty boxcars to a train.
Our train was repaired there.

We stayed in the cattle-cars.
They did not show us the museums.
From Dresden we went east to Auschwitz.

German Student (Evanston, Illinois,
August 1954, 2 a.m.):

It was like an oven,
The sidewalks were unbearable,
Asphalt popped in the street.

Unable to make it with both children,
She had to choose between them.
Afterwards her feet were amputated.

The Key

Whatever it was inside
Wanting out (and what
Was there that didn't?)
Had lost the key and couldn't
Find a window. Dear woman,
They raged for you, for themselves,
And, perhaps, most for me.
Though they chased every
Fantasy that flitted past,
Gnawed every bone in
Their dungeon, and in their
Madness saw many lovely images,
Yours was steadier than a flame
In a closed room. Your face
Was what it always is,
Spectrum of what you are,
Study in courtesy and grace
Bathed in the kind of light
A painter waits for all morning
Only to find it shifting through
Such subtle degrees he cannot catch
The tone: it will not stay.
But yours stays. And of all
The images inside this gothic room,
Only yours has dimension, only
Yours draws these animate fragments
Into a hand, an extension
Of a sentient being whose fingers
Know how to turn a knob or open

Shutters. Sometimes it happens
With a look, even a memory of
A look, sometimes with a touch.
Sometimes our bodies stretched
Their full length occasion such
A happy clatter of openings
I can close my eyes and feel
Sunlight flooding the house.

The Dreamers

(For Frances)

I lie awake beside you,
My weighted eyelids sprung into a stare.
Even asleep, you are a garden.
Outside, the winter calms, the snow half gone.
Although the sky appears to be dawn-colored,
I know it is too early for dawn.

And I ask what dreams keep time
With your deep breathing
While your body dreaming flesh for my image
Grows greater with dreaming.
My sprung eyes scan the mercury light
For a vision to match the dreamer your body dreams.

Littoral

Once on Sunday I took my sons where the sea
Had thrown up sandbars and tidepools far out
From dry beach until the moist, wave-stripped
Littoral had bared a nereid skin of sand
I scanned with skint eyes for the scampering
Beneath it of mollusks and crustaceans
And for whatever mortared with salt spittle
The primordial architecture of minute, chimnied
Castles out of broken shells, sand, and seaweed.

We saw fish answering our motions
Skipping on top of the water, chunks of palm
Trunk like huge pine cones, sand dollars in
Tidepools reaching seaward, sea the motionless
Inconceivable eye of ageless saturation
Of life and mineral in warm shallows and on
The half-guessed ocean floor's terrain.
The rush of wave pulls back the shells with
Blackened tin can tops, pop or beer—among
Oil-tar painted rocks, chewed pilings,
And huge stones thrown up against the sea's
Thrust, now worn and barnacled. We looked:
The nereid gone, seaweed scattered like hair.

Whatever general answers I have given them,
Denied or been unable to deny, I have
Shown them where the beach drops suddenly
To dark water with waves folding and folding
Themselves on sand like thick wrinkled skin
Dissolving on contact with land—a being
More amorphous and strange than any in it
And connecting all the extremes in the sun's eye.

In the Zebra

I. Leaving Camp

The camp asleep, the bugle
waiting its breath, I walked
out on the wooden harp.
There by the music's edge
where the lake reflected no star,
I climbed the horizontals,
first to the higher,
then to the highest board,
and hovering for one moment,
for one moment bird,
dived into that other

to enter a lidless eye
never to leave the lake
though they grappled it with hooks
and all the good swimmers
put on their masks to look
for me in mine.
The sharp points slid in my slime.
No one knew me by my motion.
I swam in front of their windows,
turning the water into oxygen,
weaving my way with my body.

Through muffling water bells
ringing slow long circles the sound
of the iron tongue throbbing from
my skull lapped the land with

the continued ringing of memory
repeating the one original
stroke. I cannot tell whether
the bell that shakes my sleep is
something I have heard. The world
becoming female, I awake to water—
eel, electric, dying to live.

II. Natural Monument

Earth and the weather made it
unnaturally tall, of a substance
sand, sun, rain, and wind
could only harden and smooth.
Yet its own matter, its thought,
is that by which it shapes
itself, intrinsic action.
Its mind, immured in matter,
does not speculate
on things or men or gods,
though in its cellars,
smaller than men can imagine,
the light locked in the darkness
and the parentage of all is kept
electric. The fish inside
the plankton is the rock inside
itself. Singular, material,
all fruit, all seed,
indestructible and protean.

It is related to whatever it is
that stands at either end
of all the corridors
down which what happens dreams
and makes sealed exits yield.

III. Tableau

My son—a boy no larger than the one
on the dolphin and with
the proportions but
old—was standing by the clearing
there in the zebra
                    he did not see me
here in the bedrock.
                         He was not crying
nor laughing the trees nor grass
nor was anything except myself given
to the colorless conversation of
that small brown bird
dwarfish pedestrian
that hopped speaking slowly it
did not know how to color
the unnumbered frames drying
in one frieze
                    a stopped sundial
the sheer warm catalyst
                              whirring
over the mineral virgin
submerged in birth

the tedious fumbling certain
calculations of chance
the fins feet wings
hands, then, the final
aberration.
         He was unable
to see me unable to see
or see through the whole structure
to where I was dreaming myself
thinking my hellenistic child
an awkward cygnet among those
ordinary trees that grass listening
to that small brown bird that
could not color the nerves
devouring my body before they surfaced
into the beak and gills
of the dying zebra.

The Lives and Wars of Bunzo Minagawa

"World War II ended Saturday for
Bunzo Minagawa after 16 years of
solitude in Guam's jungles." (1961)

He talked in dreams, at home in that new world,
Shattered by ordinary jungle sounds and mended
Over and over, like a vase, into new grotesques.

He searched the sounds behind the screams of birds,
The foreign scent that sometimes filled the jungle
Of corporeal trees the wind dared not disturb.

Two years in the island maze before he knew
Which tangled vines could hide the eye of days
And settled in one place for fourteen more.

He wore the same unwashed fatigues. The pouches
Carried a dirty bandage and a brown Buddha.
Though carved from jungle wood, the Buddha confused

Perfected instincts. It answered in strange tones.
His muffled quickening caught momentum from
The pungent waves, the rise of laughing voices.

When strange to running he fell in friendly vines,
The foreign animals caught and held him down.
Suddenly the peace was over, and the old wars.

Sixteen and twenty years old. Where to begin
Again? When he was a child he played with soldiers.
Buddha? But who is Buddha among these men?

The museum displays of ivory, tiered and inlaid,
Are not like that brown Buddha that flames his eyes,
Though men would retrain, revise, and make it theirs.

The Dead Baby

Inside me has long eyelashes,
Curled up in my paunch
Without blood, food, or air.

The doctors believe he was
My siamese brother developed
Inward, the root of a skeleton
That ceased to grow.

I cannot remember when I
First noticed the tightness.
Attempts beget invention.

The day I last cried
I recall stifling a wail
That seemed just then
(As I recall it now)
Separate from my own,
An echo, really,
That never stopped.

His organs are all
Connected to mine by blocked tubes;
Otherwise, he was ideally made.

His death made my life possible.

I have begun to notice
A doubleness in people
So subtle I cannot
Separate the two;

I see the faint outline
Of a small body turned upside
Down, feet pushing
Against a continual retch.

Surgery is not possible.

3

The Tunnel

The hole   in the middle
Of the backyard   had two channels.
I ran the hose in   the longest
Two yards. The force   couldn't overflow it.
And when I turned   the hose off
The water   sank.
"Snakehole!"   the boys cried.
"A root,"   said their mother,
As the tunnel   spiralled through me
A hundred feet   down
To the edge   of the river
Of sound   between   the Devil's Hopper
And Dry Lake   (where   the water drains
Every   seventh   year
Through   a sink   to run, after
Some swervings   directly beneath us).
It comes up   as Wacissa, I think, where
Divers in caves   have found whitish-pink
Fish without eyes.   My eldest believes
The fish were once   roasted in a hidden
Cavern over continual   campfires circled
By descendants   of lost tribes—
Ichetucknee,   Miccosukee,
Apalachee—   and runaway slaves.
Some mornings   in the dry season
I think I see the smoke   drifting out.

The Book of the Dead

I lie on the ground.
The ground cries out.
The house stops beating.
Deep and quiet in the earth
A cool breath listens
Without a tongue.

Trees grown from humus
Fall heavily into it.
Houses in hills crumble.
The earth accepts them.
Inside are sons of suns.
Sleeping, I think downward
Through the Miccosukee,
Suwannee Limestone,
And Jackson Bluff formations
To the fossil speech
Of men with accents like rivers
And swamp rain and bird cry
And squirrel bark.

Down to waters cold and thick
As the movements of thought
Earth thinks with its motions.
As when at twelve I descended
Into the third room
Of the Devil's Hopper
And lay with my head in the dark

Hole that had taken men
Twenty plowlines down, room after
Winding room, into a roar
That still sounded far off;
And I heard its lapidary tongue,
In its language of pure opacity
I had no way to translate,
Telling precisely the shapes
And sizes of the earth's cavities.

The Land of Old Fields

After the latest mass murders
police scan infrared maps
for "hot spots" radiated
by decaying bodies;
they lug geiger counters
through abandoned fields listening
to the idiotstuttering, where
arrowheads lie on the ground
near bricks made by slaves,
and the names of slaveholders
who hunted Indians for bounty
are still hallowed in schoolbooks
shining with blood.

Large cats know in their paws
where they are by the felt
currents of underground rivers.
The earth has voice prints
I cannot hear even when I lie
near my father's house
with my best ear to the ground.

Snakes, cold-blooded,
spend their waking lives regulating
body temperatures. Deaf,
they hang their tongues in the night
to measure the slightest concussions
of air flowing into their mouths;
their scales decipher sound.
At night they are drawn like blood

to the best conductors:
large rocks that remember
noon sun, new grave slabs.

Fossils and tooled stones litter Apalachee.
"Tallahassee"—from Seminole—
the land of the old fields;
"Seminole"—from Creek—
they who went to a new place;
   from
      "cimarron"—American Spanish—
     wild, runaway;
   from
      "maroon"—French—
     runaway slave;
"A'palachi"—from Choctaw—
the people on the other side.
Old settlements, abandoned villages,
fathers known and unknown, scrambled
evidence, lost tongues.

Dark cat, I stealthily reenter
the country of my origin.
It does not give itself easily.
It hides its fawns. The rainbow
snake sinks its subtle spectrum
in swamps. The scarlet snake and coral
hide their red and yellow bands.
I eat its mushroom visions,
looking for passages in it never unlocked.
It will not learn my name.
My feet feel their way
by a braille my brain cannot read.
I listen, my whole body a tongue.

Bellair

Pait, pieet, pweat, the ivory-bill's
Shrill cry rips through pinewoods;
The charred eye leaps into flame;
The flame-crested head ignites the green needles.
And in the hot months, there
To the open pine-shaded woods would repair
The ladies, small sons, and daughters
Of planters and merchants. All summer long
Mockingbirds, thrashers and warblers
Sheltered in light green leaves of redbud and dogwood
Sang of how some late-blooming magnolia,
With its white fleshy flower, or persistent wisteria
Made every fragrance and bloom in the forest despair—
Wild Rose, Pine Sap, Honey-balls,
Rose-pink, Mad-dog Skullcap
    Bellair, Bellair, Bellair,
The war has sung you away with the cotton and slaves,
And the ivory-bill who watched from the highest pine
Swooped down again. *Pieeet, paieet, peet.*

They curtsied and smiled and tried to learn to sing
The formal airs of Italy and the Rhine.
They fled malaria and the dog days for games.
They played out long, innocuous pantomimes,
Half-literate in a wilderness of mosquitoes.
In the scent of turpentine boxes on slave-slashed pines,
They fluttered their fans like heavy butterflies
With dwarfed, deformed wings, while servants smiled
And scavenged the bushes to root out rattlesnake nests.
They imagined themselves nymphs in a sylvan glade
Cavorting with gods (fastidious soldiers who got
Wealth and land for killing women and children—
For Jackson, the Butcher). Call their names,
Call—

    Pait, pieet, pieet.

Christ in the Sun

(A Spanish padre is sick with fever in the New World.)

Since in our great forests we have no roads
Nor cities, we have dreamed of a land of sun
Merely; though a paradise with neither Christ
Nor a Christian is Satan's work, an illusion of lust
That stirs fantasies as fever stirs my blood
And tempts to conquest, a test for Christian man.

The primitive men we find here are, to us, new men,
Though old world men are also new here. These roads
Bewilder my brain. The vessels of my blood
Are inflamed by the naked savages and their sun.
God tempts us with false freedom; the rank lust
Of old Adam, my enemy, hopes to win me from Christ.

But I will preach them Christ! Christ! Christ!
As the stern fathers did me, from boy to man,
Until I, until they, are stronger than our lust,
Or Christ is stronger in us than these false roads—
And these pagan chants, these dances to the sun,
Like these tempers, are purged from our dark blood.

"O Father, take this darkness from my blood
And brain, make bright for me, in me, Christ's
Pure Light. The simple light of their sun
Must be our darkness. O what is man
That delusion in him can take such subtle roads
He cannot know love from a lie, faith from lust?"

They did receive us freely, despite their lust
For the flesh. Though crude, they have a gentle blood,
A child's pulse for earth and creatures. Their roads
Leave no scars. They have small property. Like Christ
They would rather give than receive. Their shamans
Say they walk in the light of two worlds, two suns.

Yet it is like Eden, this place, with its warm sun,
Its flowers, flesh, fruit, fresh streams. Is it lust
To breathe too deeply, is the faith that cools my blood
Then also false that it can enrage a man
Against such outward grace in the joined names of Christ
And that dreamed life to which death is the one road.

Here, where the one road is the sun's road,
Spain, torn between goldlust and Christ lust,
Drives its two-edged sword into every man's blood.

The Turtle's Voice

My eyes know their way
In light or dark, thicket
Or path; the ground is a well.
I hear thunderous shuffling
Like many deer running
Or a whole people forced
To walk away from their lives.

The sun is our eye. I
Hunted the turtle's voice
When the sky was blind.
Rocks on my tongue
Fell until I felt
The wind from its wings,
And a waterfall over my head
Sank claws in my brain.
Light took me away,
Its child, to children
Carrying wood, dogs
Running and barking,
Sisters berrying,
Babies on their backs,
Women gathering bark,
Old men polishing
Wood, stone, bone.
I am crazy with dream.

I walk in pinewoods,
My stomach a bird's in
A bird's talons. Deer
Crowd this place where
No one berries near
Fish-swarmed rivers.
But in my inward eye
Men in polished shells
Like locusts come and kill
The deer, uproot
Even the grape, gnaw
Bark from pines, drain
Pines of sap and hack
Them down. Sickness
Has turned them white.
They carry crossed bones
Before them and leave
The land barren. I leave
My tribal fields to look
For a new place.

I wake to find her
Standing near, come out
Of a dream, her tongue
Only half like mine;
Like the first woman and man,
Our eyes find themselves in
Each other; we have both
Turned from old gods; spirit
Flutters in silence; words
Fly out like a few birds that
Light near a man, heads
Cocked to one side:

From where did you come;
Will arrows fly from
The bushes of your eyes.
She bathes in a cold
Spring, turns the scarred
Inside of the deerskin
Inward, softside toward
Me: *you draw me*
To you, we touch, a tribe,
A new world will rise
Out of you; hands,
Shoulders, face, flint sparks
On a dry stick,
Fingers—slow, quick—soft
Breath, move, till the stick
Flames and arms like flame
Wrap our bodies, melt,
We become one flame, the sun's
Child, full of children.

Though still in an inward ear
Sobbing sings through shuffling
Children, women, men—
Infants and aged on their backs—
Some stop to bury their dead;
The long, sharp throbbing of feet
Never stops, strange wails,
Strange tongues, strange names—
Cherokee, Creek, Choctaw—
Tumble into each other.

Lake Country White

You tell me poetry has wing and tail feathers;
Mine sticks to its roost—a naked bird
Mesmerized by the thin whine of children
Gnawing at my wooden nerves with a dull blade.

Flashbacks of infants drugged by hunger
Are voiced-over by your words
Like the arms that hold them but no longer try
To brush away flies that swarm in and out
Of their nostrils, parted lips and cracked,
Sleeping eyes.

While I was seeing this, you voiced-over
Africa and Asia; and I should not have mentioned
The heavy silences of the aged
In hospital waiting rooms—
You told me not to—
Or the courtrooms of the poor
Missing a day's wages to be quizzed by
A gentle judge with a voice like yours.

You keep telling me I should fly away
To the mountains or suburbs or Disneyworld.
I sip my Taylor's Lake Country White,
Listening to you and watching my children
Playing like gazelles on a fertilized lawn.
I may be happier than you know here in Florida;
Your voice gnaws at my nerves;
Imagination sticks to its roost—a naked bird
Growing enormous and pecking at your words.

King

All night mad-eyed attack dogs you had faced
Barked down nightmare streets then suddenly hushed.
But here, gentled by grief, we stood in a thick line
Wrapping Spelman three times to glimpse your casket.
Traffic choked the city. Darkness came down
Around our imprisoned masks. The long line wound
Through the night, the next day and beyond, a twisting
Silence. *Have we survived? Did you survive*
In us? Whose voice will make the word live
Or sing us up those hot asphalt hills
Toward the innocent land our fathers dreamed?
We had wanted, at least, to touch your sleeve.
We brought both babies as to a christening,
But they grew hungry and we had to leave.

When the child in me still tries to see Jesus,
You are walking the red clay edge of blue highways,
Thousands following you into the slit eyes of small
Towns toward mastiffs whose will to kill is kept
On an orgasmic chain, and into the nation's capital
To overturn the tables (Army Intelligence ordering
Find out what 'dream' he means)—
The bulldog-faced top cop slandering your memory—
You walked into the smell of jails, the winding minds
Of southern sheriffs and were scared, but (since
They too were scared) made them your sanctuaries.
You faced that outlaw's law a thousand times
Before he slunk into the dark to shoot, sure
He did what police dogs wanted but could not do.

The world flew into Atlanta into that flow, while
The Grand Dragon, still locked in his room, listened
To tapes of your speeches for the secret of your power
(Lacking your love of learning and knowledge of love).
And Little Lester, barricaded in the governor's office
With State Police to guard his chicken guilt,
Looked out as greatness passed him and,
Again, missed his chance with mankind.
By train, plane, bus, and in old and new cars
(Alabama, Mississippi, Florida),
Headlights burning, white, black,
Old age, youth and middle filled one silence.
No other testimony can erase this.
No violence was here. Nothing against your truth.

The Tree

In the dream my mother prays without an accent
Of any kind. Her goodness answers. God tells her
He has made her strong, to be long suffering.
She is a tree; her leaves are tongues in the wind.
My mirror does not mock me. I mock it. It shows
An Ife bronze face: sharp-edged, full lips, arced
Jaws, stippled beard, almond eyes, beads of braided
Hair. I twist it into my father's: eyes that must
Lift weights to look into the eyes he cannot
Love, jowls of a blooded hound who knows his quarry;
A face like an African mask for the oak god (Oldfieldia
Africana), shoulders sloped like plow shafts. He buries
Acorns in sharecropped fields and digs up live effigies
For sons and daughters. One has seven books.
They too are effigies, heavy for me. The others
Think my books like hope—hard and empty.
The study is easy. They are full of acorns and leaves.
The hard part is being a tree whose loam must feed
Branches it knows nothing of in an air and light
That know little of loam. In the school
Of strangers, my comfortable, polite friends are
Discomforting. At home I swim in the splashing
Laughter of those with little to lose. Neighbors
Slap my back, look me over, and say, "Gaaaddamn!
You still out of jail and in school; you sho's a slow
Study." —"Child, don't listen to him. Keep on
Goin'; jes' 'member the folks you come from.
Don't forget we love ya." But my thoughts throb
Through images strange to them in a bastard speech
Half-learned, half-mine. I fear to loose my tongue

In the wind like a leaf lest its edges serrate
Friends and marry broad in atonal arrangements.
In the part where I am a squirrel, nut in teeth,
An echoing hound barks down from the tree,
"Come up! Come up!" These sequences scare me,
As if he's saying, "Keep going the way you are,"
Then, "Over here! Over here!" What he says is
"Branches increase the acorn." I try to translate:
Ends that pull away from the same center
Form a single line that curves back on itself;
All things grow in proportion to the oppositions
They can sustain within. "Pa, it stretches us both."

The Evidence

My son kept wanting a snake.
That day our walk went
to a wooded hill near the school,
where we found on a winding path,
suddenly widening,
the burned and shrivelled
plastic flesh
of toy men among
thirty or forty long
wooden match stems,
their red-and-white heads charred
where the first spurts of fire
had startled nervous hands.
The evidence lay there,
almost looking unstruck,
surrounding
soldiers dressed for a battle
more real than themselves,
several fused in a mass.
Here and there, others,
apart, were equally deformed.
Among them, unharmed,
was a lone survivor
and, beside him, one match
unstruck. I let my son
bring the survivor home
and kept the match.
We found no snake.

Now it is late,
the neighborhood is still,
I sit in the living room
run my thumbnail
through the match's head
and watch it spurt
white, blue, red
and go out.
It doesn't help.
As light after light goes out
in the thousand houses around me
a child is striking
matches in his sleep.

Iowa City, 1969
After the "Pinkville Incident"

Federal Pen

With a used injector blade,
He carved in his wrist
A relief of veins
And, being a perfectionist,
Opened his throat
With a streak of pain,
Then lay on his iron
Cot watching his moat
Become a lagoon, the concrete
Around the red lagoon
Turn into sand
Where a girl with budding breasts
Green eyes and sunburnt hair
Sang in a tremulous voice
Much as the child could hear
A folksinger raise
Jesse James, father of
David, from the Red Sea
Into a tree of forks
From whose sibling limbs
Zombie Jesus
Climbed to kiss him
With blazing six-guns.

In the Manner of V. B.: for George Seferis

Across fields of tobacco, peanuts and melons,
pine needles speak their sibilants to the green
pecans. Sand and clay roads wind their riddles
away from highways that stretch level gun-gray
lines spotted with sun-slicks. I was born
into a depression of the soul no number
of farm bungalows can hide.

Wherever I go the South wounds me.
There's a smoldering cross where the aorta
intersects history. Where ganglia were removed,
a livid impulse wove them and hung
the dark mystery of being from the curve
in my windpipe.
                        Timucua, Muskhogee, Cherokee—
                        Shenandoah, Shiloh, Atlanta—
                        Little Rock, Selma, Memphis—
every childhood scar I have named will shine
from my flesh. No matter how I burned my leg
at three, the scar remembers the missile shot
from the fire. I wore the skin of an old man.

The onion cheeks of the old minister in Chicago
wrinkled genially when he said in his British accent,
"we are careful to keep our congregation homogenous."
When I saw he was telling me what he thought I wanted
to hear, I could have wept and he would not have known
for how many of us I was grieving. Wherever I went
people unzipped and pulled out their prejudices
to make me feel at home.

After the wars when I had finished school,
I came home to the shrill cries of the bluejay,
the hammering of the red-bellied woodpecker
and the cardinal's searing flame.

What do they want, all those who believe
they know what they are and where they are from?
Someone from Salem asked if I came from Selma.
"No, from Haywire," I said, "to the south of Omega."
We give our towns names hard to forget.
He was drinking the South out of a green body.

Meanwhile, the South is travelling.
There are people in the South who drive past
sporting christianschool bumperstickers.
They look into a green lake and see a civilization
that was never anything but possibility.

When my car broke down in Alabama,
my family stranded on the freeway,
the mechanic in the pickup who stopped and fixed it
with a used part he had to make a trip for
wouldn't let me pay him, and, as part
of his hospitality, he even pointed to a green hill
nearby, where the KKK once burned three men.

In Illinois, north of Springfield, we stopped
to gas the U-Haul and my five-year-old told
the attendant "we're moving to Florida."
"Nuthin ther," said the Yankee, "but niggers
and gators." Before we left Iowa, a poet's
wife, from New England, said how scared
her husband was when stopped in Louisiana

for speeding. "He said he'll never go there
again," she said. "Right," I told her, "they
break your fingers. In Evanston," I said
"a police lieutenant only called my friend
a stupid ass for having a Southern accent."
Light breaks where no sun shines: "O,
O," she called across the room, "Richard,
come here and hear what he says." And
the Arizona land salesman from Minneapolis
was entertaining our table at the sales dinner
with how he kept blacks out of neighborhoods
in St. Paul and Tucson when I remarked on how
much he looked like cowpie. After he left,
the quiet Iowa couple across the table said how
embarrassed they were and glad I'd said something.

The South keeps travelling. We are cutting down
forests to build surreal suburbs far from the heart
of the city, selling swamps that look like shrewd
pickings, trading dreams we were stalled in.
People are buying our grief.

Wherever I go the South wounds me.
Crosses on white churches glint in the Indian sun—
fields, mountains, lakes; alligators, deer
disappear into the names of my scars.
The dark lump in my throat revolves on its rope.
The cardinal's insistent, raucous arguments
grow faint in my ears.

I'm really from a place near Natchez called Blues,
I told the man with the empty green body.
You have to go through it to get to Mardi Gras.

To a Friend

Later that summer we climbed Iztaccihuatl
(The Sleeping Woman), her twin peaks still alive
but dormant. At twelve thousand feet, drowsy.
I slept in the deep soft grass of a green slope
While you, Roberto and the others pushed toward
Her dancing snowcap. On the way down you woke me.
And between Zacopoaxtla and one of its seven
Villages, when I grew tired of carrying piggy-
Back the lame Indian boy who adopted us
And thought he ought to walk, you carried him.
We walked ground never pillaged
By Spaniard, settler, nor cavalry—Indian earth.

We had chosen you capitán, but your fever rose
(From dysentery or from some mountain stream,
We thought at first)—then your appendix burst
There at the feet of the Sierra Madres.
You were reading Gandhi, thinking of peace.
You read in the hospital the rest of the summer
While we patched old schools, painted, taught,
And played games with the children and town sports.
Then we both went home, hitchhiking from San Antone
Until you split northward from Baton Rouge.
In the incredible heat of that southern road,
We stopped twice for doctors to dress your wound.

You wrote from Antioch of long introspections.
I pictured you sitting, reading, in spaced woods,
Your thoughts filling them. You were my Woolman:
Sharp-edged, clean light, without a metaphysics.
On your way abroad, you wrote from New York, jailed
For joining a picket line, still trying to dress
The volcanic festerings.
We met in Chicago (you had still not crossed the ocean),
Then I got a picture of your wife and daughter
From Oakland. Then lost track. Hank, we move so much.
When craters erupt, I think of your deep quiet.
Are you still in the States? Still out on bail?

The Ivory-Billed Woodpecker

"It lived on a restricted diet of wood-boring
larvae that infest dead and dying trees of a
certain age and thus required large tracts of
mature forest for living space."

The ivory-bill scans swamps.
His large beak stabs the air.
The interstate's red incision,
Stretching from the Ochlocknee to
The Wacissa, from the Aucilla
To the Chipola, slowly turns black.
In the widening circle of his flight,
The line like the lid of an eye
Lengthens as it narrows
And closes on him. Okefenokee,
Big Cypress—
    "pait, pait-pait"
(Audubon said),
He circles burial mounds unearthed
Beneath a chief's floor.
For thousands of miles believers
Look for the last surviving
Ivory-bill, tracing rumored sightings
(the Singer Wilderness,
The Big Thicket), sifting
Piles of chips sheered in huge
Swipes by his airhammer beak.

The unfinished interstate sinks
In the vanishing swamp and the swirl
Of the sun's heat. He dips
Toward illusion, the slime
Of green water (there are three,
Four of them, pileated, not ivory-
Bills; smaller, charred beak in
Each flaming head. Nor is it water.)
A green front-end loader
Starts with a loud chirr to clear
Topsoil, tree, and more at a time.
From a tree nearby, the birds look
Out of alternate sides of their
Heads and fly away,
The distorted landscape
In their half-round eyes,
Ignited trees rising.

Driving at Night

Sitting under a bulb hung in a bowl-shaped shade,
You hold your glasses between your face
        and the yellow legal pad
On legs propped on the desk and see in the lens
Two albino eyes slightly crossed.

The eyes look at you, like distant headlights in
The rearview mirror, milky irises and incandescent
Pupils, and when you move the glasses the eyes dilate
Or contract, as the beams fall back in the mirror or
        overtake.

Occasionally you glimpse an animal beside the road
        in the grass
As your beams or the moon's glint from its eyes.
There could be a man or child lying there, hiding
Or hurt, unable to cry out, even dead, but watching.
        You swear it's
A possum or coon, though you know it may be a cat.

They are only concave/convex reflectors, yet
        the symmetrical
Spacing is that of eyes—not fireflies, tincans or
        bottlecaps—
You'll never know what kind. You look up at pupils
Scattered without irises in the night sky, turn on
        the radio or start to hum
Or sing all the songs you ever knew, surprised how
Many there are and how many formulas you've stored
        away. The more

You remember, the more awake you become; and in
      the echo
Chamber of your car you dilate into incandescence.

At three a.m., between occasional semis, your brights
Like unfolding snowdrifts turn to gray slush as you plow
It off. It buries a desolate house whose dim lit window
Reminds you of stories you told or heard as a child,
Or of houses in which you have lived but never been.

When you have ground asphalt to slush, thrown it off,
Come again to streets whose names you know, to turn
      into your own
Driveway, and forgotten the perfect ovals you saw
Projected through your glasses but not yours,
The cyclopean bulb will still hang from your ceiling
By a thin pair of insulated nerves you imagine hum

      He didn't find the quack, crack, clack
      They call the rising sun, way down yond
      In the paw paw patch black flax is my
      True love's hair, a hundred coachwhips long.

You put down the glasses and yellow pad, go to bed,
Close, and the opaque road begins to form, open
And fall away, blurring the edges in the grass, and you
Drive down the road where houses you pass, and know,
Are places you do not know you are going but do.

About the author

Van Brock was born in 1932 on a farm in Georgia—not far from Tallahassee, where with his wife and children he has lived since 1970. He is a professor of English in the Writing Program at Florida State University and has also taught writing workshops in the F. S. U. London Study Center, at Oglethorpe College, and at the University of Iowa. He has a B. A. from Emory University and M. A., M. F. A., and Ph. D. degrees from Iowa. He has been a volunteer worker in Mexico, a social worker in Chicago, Atlanta, and Houston, and a reporter in North Carolina.

These poems appeared originally between 1964 and 1979 in journals such as *North American Review, The New Yorker,* and *Southern Review.* Brock's previous collections are *Final Belief, Weighing the Penalties,* and *Spelunking;* the last of these was also a special issue of *New Collage.* In 1977, Brock was the first featured poet in *Poets in the South.* His poems have been anthologized in *New Voices in American Poetry, New Southern Poets, 1976/Young American Poets* (in Japanese translation) and two Borestone Mountain Poetry Awards annuals. His awards include a Borestone Prize, a Rockefeller Fellowship from the F. S. U. Center for the Study of Southern Culture and Religion, a Creative Writing Fellowship from the Fine Arts Council of Florida, and six first prizes, ranging from the 1964 Kansas City Contests to the 1977 Florida Poetry Prize. He has been a resident of the MacDowell Colony, the Ossabaw Island project, and the Hambidge Center.

Brock is also known for his encouragement of other poets—in his workshops and as sponsor of *Sundog* magazine, director of the Apalachee Poetry Center, and former coordinator of Poets-in-the-Schools and Poets-in-the-Prisons programs. His Anhinga Press publishes anthologies of poetry, a poetry chapbook series, and full-length poetry books. As poetry editor of *National Forum: The Phi Kappa Phi Journal,* he has published promising younger poets along with the more established.

Photo: Mary McCutchan

Van K. Brock